21st
Century
Skills Library

COOL CAREERS
AIR TRAFFIC CONTROLLER

NANCY ROBINSON MASTERS

Published in the United States of America by
Cherry Lake Publishing, Ann Arbor, Michigan
www.cherrylakepublishing.com

Content Adviser
Paul VJ Drechsel, Assistant Professor, Aviation, University of North Dakota

Credits
Photos: Cover and pages 1 and 26, ©Cultura RM/Alamy; page 4, ©Lars Lindblad/
Shutterstock, Inc.; page 6, ©Petronilo G. Dangoy Jr./Shutterstock, Inc.; page 9,
©iStockphoto.com/mayo; page 10, ©Jirsak/Shutterstock, Inc.; pages 12 and 28,
©vario images GmbH & Co.KG/Alamy; page 14, ©iStockphoto.com/picturedesigner;
page 17, ©MarchCattle/Shutterstock, Inc.; page 18, ©Stock Connection Blue/
Alamy; page 20, ©Lisa F. Young/Shutterstock, Inc.; page 23, ©iStockphoto.com/
GeorgeClerk; page 24, ©Visions of America, LLC/Alamy

Library of Congress Cataloging-in-Publication Data
Masters, Nancy Robinson.
  Air traffic controller/by Nancy Robinson Masters.
    p. cm.—(Cool careers)
  Includes bibliographical references and index.
  ISBN-13: 978-1-60279-940-0 (lib. bdg.)
  ISBN-10: 1-60279-940-7 (lib. bdg.)
  1. Air traffic control—Vocational guidance—Juvenile literature.
  2. Air traffic controllers—Juvenile literature. I. Title. II. Series.
  TL725.3.T7M363 2010
  387.7'40426023—dc22   2010000693

Cherry Lake Publishing would like to acknowledge
the work of The Partnership for 21st Century Skills.
Please visit *www.21stcenturyskills.org* for more information.

Printed in the United States of America
Corporate Graphics Inc.
July 2010
CLFA07

COOL CAREERS

TABLE OF CONTENTS

CHAPTER ONE
FROM BONFIRES TO SATELLITES

"Would you like a pillow?" Coach Gwen asked each of the four members of the Central Elementary School All-Star Relay Team as they boarded Flight 520.

Air traffic controllers are responsible for providing information to pilots before takeoff and after landing.

"No thanks, Coach. I'm too excited to sleep!" Vee Jackson replied.

"Me too! I've never flown on an airplane before," Denise Martinez said as she buckled into a seat next to a window.

Sam Berry pressed his nose against the window on the opposite side of the aisle and counted out loud, "One, two, three, four, five! There are five airplanes holding short of the runway and our airplane hasn't even left the terminal."

"Holding what?" Vee asked.

"Holding short. That means waiting before taxiing out onto the runway for takeoff," Sam explained.

"How will our pilots know when it's our turn to take off?" Maurice Macon asked. "How will they know when it's our turn to land?"

"I've been wondering the same things," Denise whispered. She did not want Coach Gwen to know she was afraid the pilot flying the airplane might get lost. If the pilot got lost, she and her teammates might not make it to the Elementary All-Star Relay Race in time to compete.

Sam grinned. "Don't worry. My dad is an **air traffic control (ATC) specialist**. He and all the people he works with in the air traffic control system will help us get to the competition. They are an all-star relay team just like us."

■ ■ ■

The United States air traffic system is the safest in the world. An air traffic controller's job is to provide information and instructions to pilots in order to

- help airplanes move quickly and efficiently in the air and on the ground;
- separate airplanes to avoid collisions;
- help airplanes move safely at all times, in the air and on the ground.

Pilots rely on the information air traffic controllers provide to taxi, take off, fly, and land safely.

The pilot in command of an airplane is responsible for making the decisions about the airplane's operation. Pilots use information and instructions provided by air traffic controllers to taxi, take off, fly, and land safely. Every year, 700 million passengers are carried safely through the skies. Flight 520 is one of more than 87,000 flights made each day by **commercial airliners**, private airplanes, and military aircraft traveling these invisible highways.

21ST CENTURY CONTENT

One of the most important technologies for air traffic controllers is the Global Positioning System (GPS). GPS is a U.S. satellite navigation system. Satellites circling Earth send signals that provide immediate, accurate information about things such as weather and air traffic. Controllers use this information to reduce flight congestion and delays. In this way, controllers are helping save millions of gallons of aviation fuel each year!

The air traffic control system is a huge spiderweb of people, equipment, and services. This system supports safe and efficient flights all over the world. To do this, everyone must be able to work together. For example, the services provided by air traffic controllers in Walla Walla, Washington, are almost the same services provided by air traffic control specialists in Wagga Wagga, Australia.

Sam's dad works for the **Federal Aviation Administration** as part of the air traffic control system in the United States. There were no controllers in the United States when airplanes began carrying the mail in 1920. There were no **navigation aids** along the routes. Airmail pilots often got lost and could not fly at night. Concerned citizens built bonfires at landing fields near towns. These bonfires were the first step toward today's modern system of **airways**.

Lighted beacons replaced the bonfires. These were lamps on top of towers 51 feet (15.54 meters) high. By 1923 there were 289 beacon towers between Chicago, Illinois, and Cheyenne, Wyoming. The towers' lights rotated every 10 seconds, making them appear to be flashing. These lights made it possible for airplanes to carry mail across the country at night. The beacons were used to mark airport locations and routes for airplanes to follow.

Beacons using radio beams to guide pilots replaced the light beacons. In 1935, the first **air traffic control tower** was established in Newark, New Jersey. Two-way radio made it possible for controllers on the ground to talk with pilots in the air. This was a great improvement from the

A lineman signals to the pilot to stop after the air traffic controller in the control tower tells the pilot where to park.

days when people on the ground could only communicate with pilots by waving flags!

World War II (1939–1945) brought incredible new technology that allowed airplanes to fly higher, faster, and farther. Women began working as air traffic controllers for the first time. The war also brought the discovery of radar, or radio

detection and ranging. A radar transmitter sends out invisible radio waves. When the radio waves hit a solid object,
they bounce back. A radar receiver receives the waves as they
bounce back. A screen displays the object against which
the radio waves bounced. Radar can be used to identify the
location, altitude, direction of movement, and speed of moving objects such as airplanes.

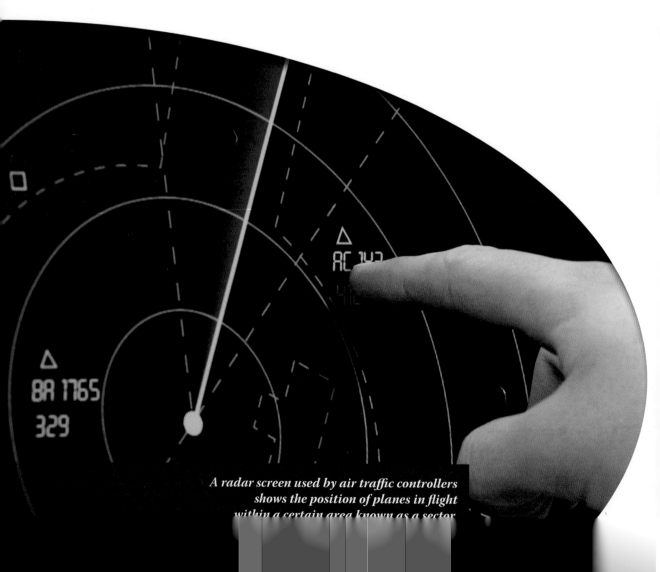

*A radar screen used by air traffic controllers
shows the position of planes in flight
within a certain area known as a sector.*

In 1952, passengers began flying on aircraft with jet engines. The Jet Age had begun! Jet engines allowed larger airplanes to fly longer distances. By 1958, more people were traveling across the Atlantic Ocean in airplanes than on ships. More airplanes carrying more passengers increased the need for more ATC workers around the world.

The International Civil Aviation Organization (ICAO), a special agency of the United Nations, was formed in 1947. Members of the ICAO come from 190 countries. They agree on the air traffic rules that their countries follow for safe, secure air travel.

Computers brought the Age of Automation to air traffic control. Computers, **simulators**, and satellite technology are bringing challenges and change to air traffic control. One thing that has not changed is the need for new air traffic control specialists. They will be needed to help ensure the safe, efficient, and orderly flow of airplanes through the sky.

CHAPTER TWO
TEAMWORK

Jim Sass has spent 10 years as an air traffic control specialist. Jim is one member of the relay team that will help Coach Gwen and the students aboard Flight 520 get to their competition. Jim works 40 hours a week at an

Each air traffic controller in a control tower has certain duties as part of the air traffic team.

Air Route Traffic Control Center (ARTCC). The ARTCC operates 24 hours a day, 7 days a week. Air traffic controllers work rotating shifts. This means he sometimes works at night, on weekends, and on holidays.

"There are about 7,000 airplanes in the air over the United States at all times. Being an air traffic controller is like carrying the baton in a relay race. We each do our job, then pass the baton to the next controller on the relay team.

"Some of us work in tall towers with windows that allow us to see in all directions at airports. Others work in dark rooms filled with radar screens. All of us work together to make air travel as safe as possible."

Let's meet some of the other members of the air traffic control relay team for Flight 520:

Kevin is the *ground controller*. He notifies the pilot when it is safe for the aircraft to be pushed away from the terminal. Then the airplane joins the line for takeoff. The ground controller gives the pilot a location for Flight 520 to hold (wait) for takeoff.

Pam is the *tower controller*. She keeps up with all of the airplanes taking off and landing at the airport. The tower controller advises the pilot when it is safe for the airplane to enter the runway and take off.

LaShaun is next, as the *departure controller*. He makes sure other airplanes do not create a hazard as Flight 520 takes off and climbs.

Jim, the *en route controller*, will provide information and directions to Flight 520 after it departs. Flight 520 will be one of 30 airplanes Jim will provide services for in his sector. A sector is a specific area of airspace.

"The airplanes in my sector fly at different speeds, altitudes, and directions. When Flight 520 leaves my sector, the next en route controller will be responsible for providing the services."

Air traffic controllers work in a room with windows all around at the top of the control tower. This room is called the cab.

LEARNING & INNOVATION SKILLS

International Civil Aviation Organization (ICAO) members agree to use English for all flight communications. Rio de Janeiro, Brazil, has been chosen as the location for the 2016 Summer Olympics. What do you think would happen if all of the pilots flying airplanes from other countries to Brazil and all of the air traffic controllers along the way did not use a common language for communications?

During Jim's shift he may have multiple duties. He might be operating the printer that prints flight progress strips. These strips of paper contain all the information about each flight being served by the Center. This includes where the plane took off from and where it will finally land. Jim might be providing information to other controllers about equipment or weather problems. He could be training a new controller at the same time.

Anthony is the *approach controller* at the airport where Flight 520 is going to land. He takes responsibility for the airplane from the final en route controller. The approach controller organizes all of the airplanes coming into an airport.

Flight 520 will flow into line behind flights bringing other teams to the relay competition.

The approach controller will transfer control of Flight 520 to the tower controller for landing. After landing, the ground controller takes over again. The relay is complete when the airplane reaches the arrival gate at the terminal.

"Coach Gwen and the students never see me or any of the other controllers during their trip," Jim explains. "Air traffic controllers are the invisible relay team of the airways."

Some air traffic controllers work as flight service specialists, supplying information and assisting pilots in emergencies. Others work at the Air Traffic Control System Command Center in Herndon, Virginia. Controllers at the Command Center plan ways to prevent congestion problems before they happen. They focus on problems that could cause congestion at airports such as Hartsfield-Jackson International Airport in Atlanta, Georgia. Controllers at this airport handle 2,600 flights a day. This airport experiences more air traffic than any other airport in the world!

Controllers train for emergencies. They must stay calm and work together, especially in an emergency. The best example of this happened after terrorists attacked the United States on September 11, 2001. In less than 3 hours, controllers successfully directed the safe landings of about 5,000 airplanes.

"It's great to be part of the ATC team," Jim says. "It's cool to be in control."

Passengers on airliners such as the Boeing 747 never see the team of air traffic control specialists who are an important part of their flight.

CHAPTER THREE
IN CONTROL

Boeing Tower: "Piper 7787 Foxtrot cleared for takeoff, runway 13 right, fly Mercer departure."

Pilot: "Piper 7787 Foxtrot cleared for takeoff, rolling."

Air traffic controllers in some locations use information on strips of paper to track each flight. More and more locations are using computers for flight tracking.

This is what you might hear if you were listening to the conversation between an air traffic controller and the pilot of a private airplane. Air traffic controllers provide services to pilots no matter how big or small their airplanes may be.

The Federal Aviation Administration expects to hire 13,000 new air traffic controllers between 2010 and 2018. Most of these new hires will have gone to school to learn about ATC. The FAA approves colleges and universities through its Air Traffic Collegiate Training Initiative (AT-CTI). These colleges offer FAA-approved courses to help prepare workers for ATC careers. Air traffic controller jobs, however, do not necessarily require a college degree. You do not have to be a pilot, have perfect vision, or know how to talk in aviation code like the Boeing tower controller and the pilot. You can apply if you

- have worked for 3 years at any job or have attended college for 4 years;
- are between 18 and 30 years old;
- pass medical and drug screening tests;
- pass a security clearance exam to make sure you're a good U.S. citizen;
- pass the pre-application test.

The pre-application test will show how well you can read, write, and speak English. The test will also determine if you can think and work quickly to solve many different kinds of problems. Good reading, math, and science skills are important. It will take about 8 hours to complete the test.

If you are hired, you will attend a training program at the FAA Academy in Oklahoma City. The program lasts between 7 and 15 weeks. Some of the things you learn include

Trainees at the FAA Academy need good reading, writing, and study skills in order to pass tests.

- aviation terms and codes;
- FAA rules and guidelines;
- weather conditions as they apply to flight;
- how to use ATC computers and radar equipment;
- skills for being a good team member.

 LIFE & CAREER SKILLS

Not all countries use the same methods as the United States to hire and train air traffic controllers. For example, all air traffic control in Brazil is operated by the Brazilian military. No matter how they are hired or trained, all air traffic controllers around the world must be able to
- speak clearly and calmly;
- listen carefully;
- work as a team member;
- follow rules completely;
- make good decisions quickly;
- memorize information easily;
- write neatly;
- solve problems quickly.
  How many of these skills do you have?

While you are at the Academy, you will be given "pass or fail" tests. For example, you might be asked to use a pencil and piece of paper to draw from memory all the invisible airways in a certain area of airspace. Or, you may be asked to quickly solve problems without the help of a computer or calculator. If you do not pass these tests, you will not be allowed to continue attending the Academy.

After graduation from the FAA Academy, you may spend 2 to 4 years completing extra training. This may be on the job or in classrooms. Working with experienced controllers is the best way to prepare for the responsibilities of a fully-qualified controller.

Air traffic controllers in the United States earn good salaries for their hard work. Beginning controllers earn about $45,000 per year. Experienced controllers can sometimes earn more than $160,000. A number of things, such as location and years of experience, determine exact salaries. For example, an experienced controller working in a tower at a major airport may earn more money than a beginning controller working in a tower at an airport with fewer aircraft operations.

Controllers must have 25 years of active service in order to retire. They may also choose to retire after working for 20 years when they become 50 years old. Air traffic controllers must retire when they are 56 years old except in very rare cases.

The FAA Academy's training program is followed by on-the-job training in towers or at other air control facilities.

CHAPTER FOUR
2018 AND BEYOND

Do you like using computers? Do you want to help protect the environment? Perhaps your family has a cell phone that you use to display maps and find directions. If so, you might enjoy working as part of the Next Generation

Signals received from satellites circling Earth will be a major part of the air traffic control system technology of the future.

Air Transportation System. This history-making project known as "NextGen" is already underway. More and more people and cargo will be moving through the airways. NextGen will use the latest technology to meet these increasing air traffic control demands. The plan is designed by the FAA to improve safety and protect the environment.

NextGen technology moves away from ground-based radar to satellite navigation. The FAA believes this change will reduce flight time, save fuel, and reduce noise. Much of this technology will make air traffic control systems more accurate. For example, satellite-based technology updates data every second. This is much faster than radar, which updates every 4 to 12 seconds. Even in these few seconds, an aircraft can travel a great distance.

Innovations in weather forecasting and communications will mean that airports and runways are built in new ways. NextGen equipment will provide pilots with information and services that are currently provided by air traffic controllers. Incredibly detailed virtual simulators are being installed at airports including Hartsfield-Jackson in Atlanta. These simulators can model any airport under any condition at any time. This will make it possible to train new controllers better and faster.

Some people do not think NextGen is a good idea. They feel the plan will cost too much and not work well.

For example, some airlines and airports think the new equipment will be too expensive. Some air traffic controllers think more controllers will be needed for NextGen to work.

The FAA will be looking for students graduating in 2018 and beyond for air traffic control. Here are some ways you can sharpen your skills to help you prepare:

Cooperation, observation, and organization skills used by air traffic controllers today will also be needed by controllers in the future.

Cooperate with others when you are given a team assignment. Don't expect someone else to do your part for you. Make sure you complete the assignment.

Observe details about places you go all the time. What color is the roof on your school? How many steps does it take for you to walk from the cafeteria to the library? Which direction is the gym from your homeroom?

Newspapers, magazines, and books are important sources for information. Don't limit your reading and research about any subject to the Internet.

Take time to think before you answer a question. Make sure you give the best answer.

Remember by writing things down. Then reread what you write at least three times. Writing and rereading will help you remember.

Organize your desk, notebook, backpack, locker, and closet so you can always find your things quickly.

Listen to yourself speak on a recorder. Ask others if they can understand every word you say. Practice making each word clear.

Learn about other countries and cultures.

Explore opportunities to visit an airport. You may discover there is one nearby that you did not know about. Hint: Not all airports have control towers.

Regularly exercise.

Students who prepare will be ready for takeoff!

LEARNING & INNOVATION SKILLS

The National Air Traffic Controllers Association (NATCA) is an organization of air traffic controllers in the United States. Some other countries have similar organizations. One thing these organizations do is encourage students to prepare today for career opportunities in the air traffic system of the future. Some NATCA members do this by speaking at career day programs at schools. What other ways can you suggest for students to learn about air traffic control careers?

Would you like to work as an air traffic controller?

SOME WELL-KNOWN PEOPLE IN AIR TRAFFIC CONTROL

Luis Walter Alvarez (1911–1988) invented systems to make air traffic control safer and more efficient. He was awarded the 1968 Nobel Prize in physics for his work.

Archie William League (1907–1986) was the first air traffic controller in the United States. In 1929 he worked at the St. Louis airfield waving flags to signal pilots.

Almer Stillwell "Mike" Monroney (1902–1980) was a senator from Oklahoma who wrote the law to create the Federal Aviation Administration. The FAA training academy in Oklahoma City is named the Mike Monroney Aeronautical Center in his honor.

Jacqueline L. "Jacque" Smith (1931–) was one of the first women to work as an air traffic controller. She and controller Sue Mostert Townsend started an organization in 1978 called Professional Women Controllers.

Sir Robert Alexander Watson-Watt (1892–1973) was a Scottish scientist considered to be the inventor of radar.

GLOSSARY

air traffic control specialist (AIR TRAF-ik kuhn-TROHL SPESH-uh-list) a person trained to provide information and services to pilots on the ground and in the air

air traffic control tower (AIR TRAF-ik kuhn-TROHL TOU-ur) a tall building at an airport where air traffic controllers work

airways (AIR-wayz) invisible flight paths (highways) in the sky

commercial airliners (kuh-MUR-shuhl AIR-lye-nurz) planes that carry paying passengers at scheduled times

Federal Aviation Administration (FED-ur-uhl ay-vee-AY-shuhn ad-min-uh-STRAY-shuhn) the United States agency responsible for aviation

innovations (in-uh-VAY-shuhnz) new ways of doing things

navigation aids (nav-uh-GAY-shuhn AYDZ) signals and markers used to guide airplanes

simulators (SIM-yuh-lay-turz) models used for training and practice

FOR MORE INFORMATION

BOOKS

Masters, Nancy Robinson. *Airplanes*. Ann Arbor, MI: Cherry Lake Publishing, 2009.

Spilsbury, Richard. *At the Airport*. Chicago: Heinemann-Raintree, 2009.

WEB SITES

Federal Aviation Administration—Aviation Career Education (ACE)
www.faa.gov/education/student_resources/ace_camps
Watch a cool video about aviation camps for students.

Philadelphia International Airport—Kid's Corner
www.phl.org/kids_alphabet.html
Learn the aviation alphabet used by controllers and pilots.

Smithsonian National Air and Space Museum—America by Air
www.nasm.si.edu/exhibitions/gal102/americabyair
Fly across the United States during different time periods. Explore aviation and air traffic control history! This is one of the author's favorite Web sites.

21ST CENTURY SKILLS LIBRARY

INDEX

ABOUT THE AUTHOR

Nancy Robinson Masters is a private pilot and the author of more than 30 books, including books about aviation. She and her husband Bill use air traffic control services when they fly to places where Nancy presents visiting author programs for students and staff development workshops for teachers. You can find out more about Nancy at *www.NancyRobinsonMasters.com*.